101 Uses of a Dead Kindle

101 Uses of a Dead Kindle

Adrian Searle
and Judith Hastie

FREIGHT
BOOKS

Published in the UK October 2012
Freight Books
49-53 Virginia Street
Glasgow, G1 1TS
www.freightbooks.co.uk

A CIP catalogue reference for this book is available from the British Library

ISBN 978-1-9087540-7-3

Designed by Freight
Printed and bound by Bell and Bain, Glasgow

Introduction

The Kindle is now one of the most iconic consumer objects in our culture. Small, compact and ergonomic, they can be spotted on buses and trains, planes and ships, at the beach and by the pool, in the park and coffee shop, in the staff canteen, pretty much everywhere.

Estimates suggest over 2m Kindles have been sold in the UK over the last three years, with exciting new models and continued demand forecast for the years ahead. Everyone is enjoying the novelty and convenience of carrying a library of books in their briefcase or handbag. While bestsellers are available at a discount, and online promotions offer books for pennies not pounds, there are countless classics available for nothing. No one can deny that the humble e-reader is changing the way we buy and read books.

101 Uses of a Dead Kindle is a celebration of the Kindle's iconic status, taking a sideways look and what happens when, eventually, your beloved Kindle dies.

Here are 101 beautiful, imaginative and hilarious cartoons showing all the different ways you can recycle (or up-cycle) your Kindle, no matter how weird, ludicrous and extraordinary.

101 Uses of a Dead Kindle will become, we hope, a classic guide for Kindle owners everywhere.

Chapter 1:
Decorative

1. Shoulder pad

2. Sideburn

3. Epaulette

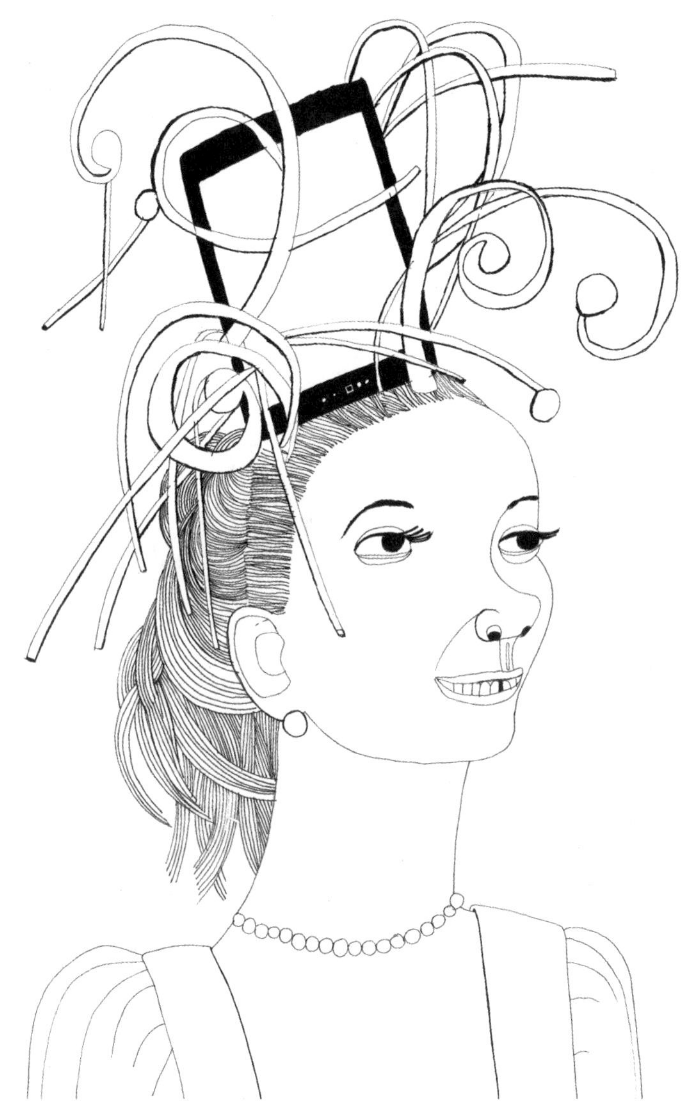

4. Fascinator

5. Fan

6. Earring

7. Sporran

8. Hairstyle

9. Bunting

10. Christmas decoration

11. African lip plate

Chapter 2:
Recreational

12. S & M paddle

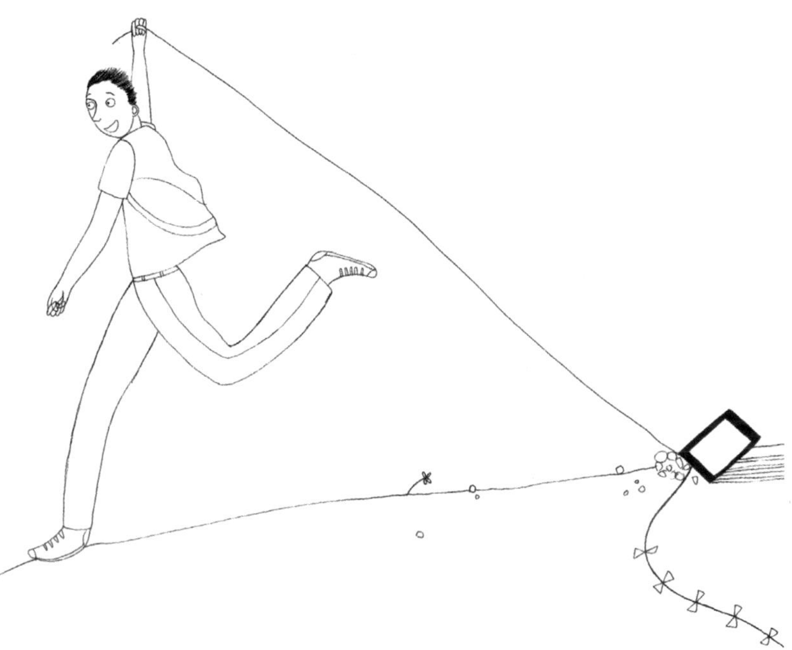

13. Kite

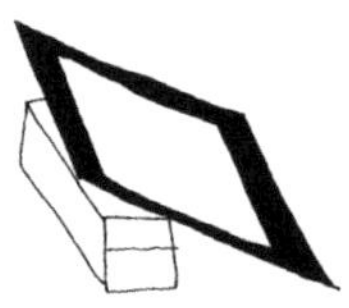

14. Skateboard ramp

15. Pharmaceutical preparation surface

16. Canoe paddle

17. Objet d'art

18. Personal massager

19. Skimming stone

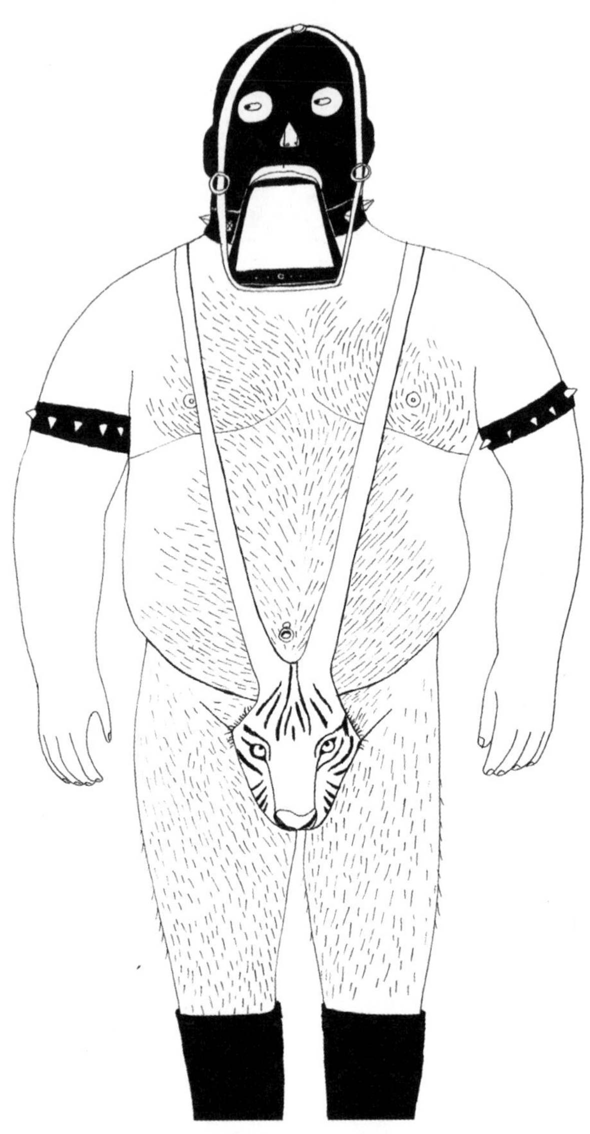

20. Gimp gag

21. Beer mat

22. Pedalo paddle

Chapter 3:

Personal Grooming

23. Tongue scraper

24. Cut-throat razor

25. Hot stones therapy

26. Toupée

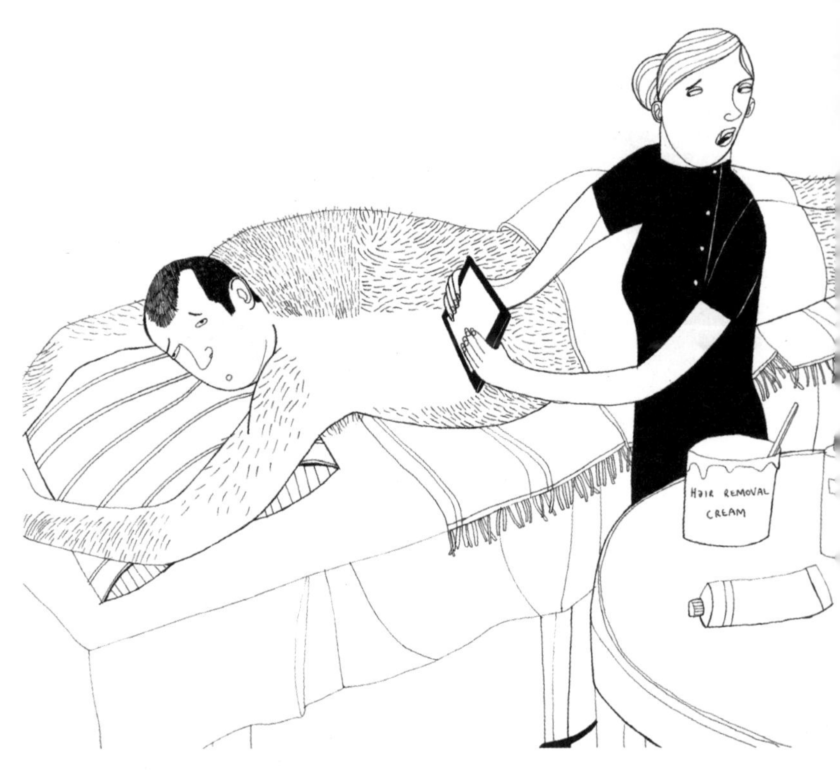

27. Exfoliator

Chapter 4: Animals

28. Litter tray scoop

29. Pet toboggan

30. Horse blinkers

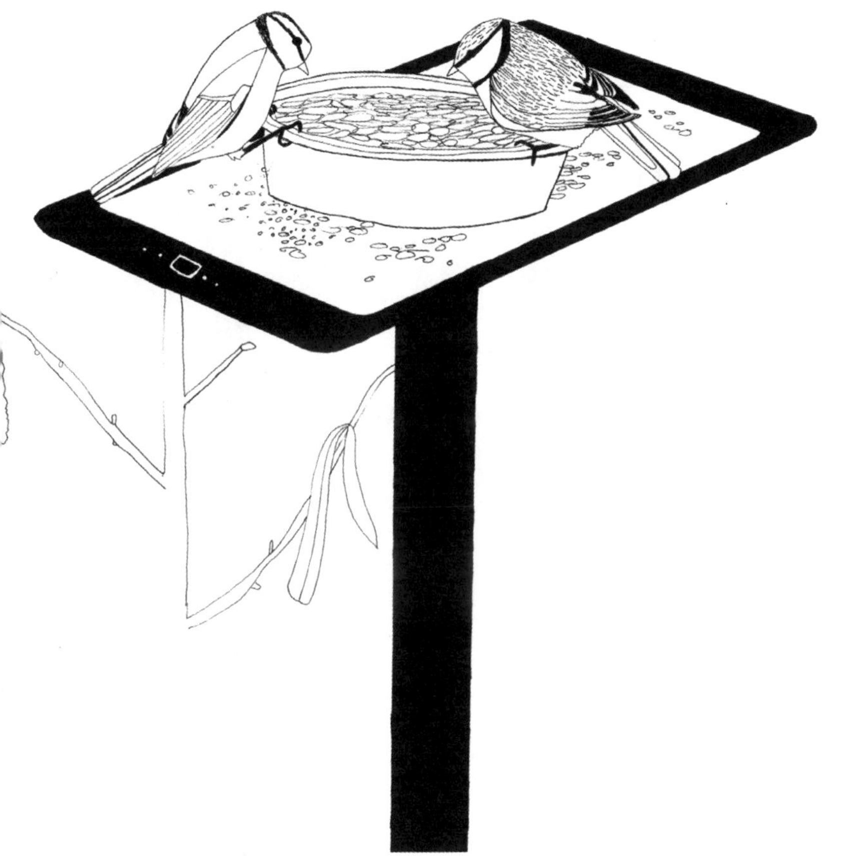

31. Bird table

32. Dog chew

33. Mouse raft

34. Cat umbrella

35. Ramp

36. Roadkill scraper

Chapter 5:
At work

37. Hostess trolley

38. Midwife baby slapper

39. Sushi tray

40. Chopping board

41. Spatula

42. Advertising sign

43. Clipboard

44. Croupier chip rake

45. Headphone

46. Plough blade

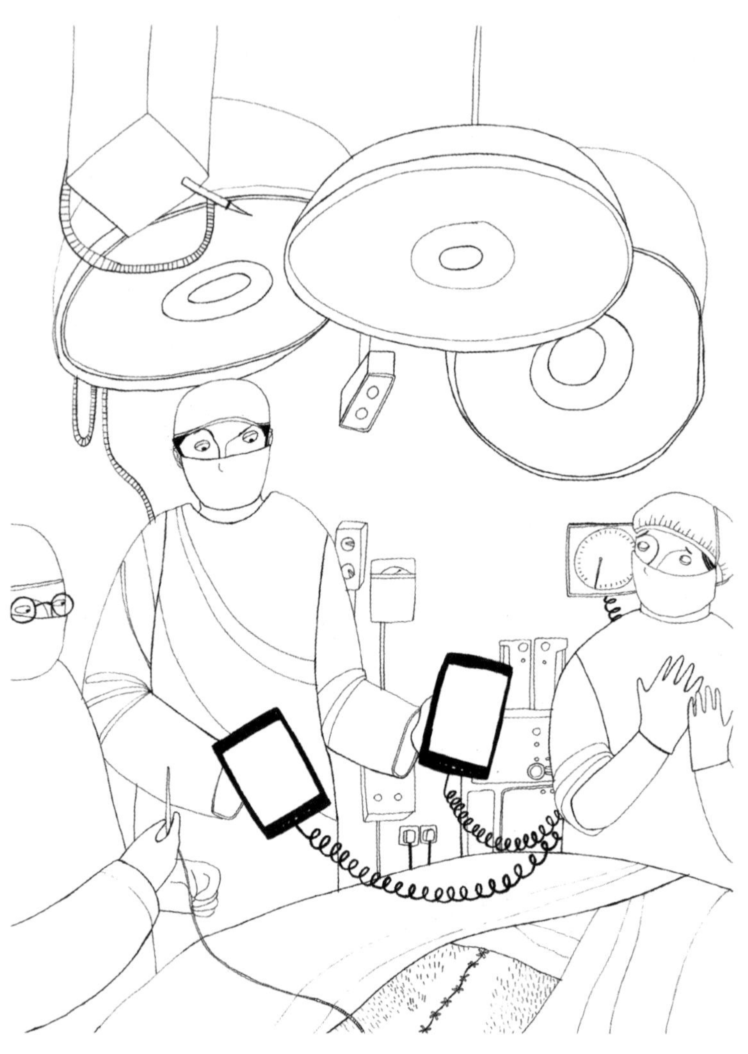

47. Defibrillator paddle

Chapter 6:
Sporting

48. Golf visor

49. Cricket box

50. Swimming float

51. Shin pad

52. Frisbee

53. Table tennis bat

54. Shooting clay

55. Flipper

56. Knee pad

57. Ice skate blade

Chapter 7:
Creative

58. Artist's palette

59. Music stand

60. Banjo

61. Chisel

62. Castanet

63. Clapper board

Chapter 8:
Things to wear

64. Eye patch

65. Snow shoe

66. Mortarboard

67. Elizabethan ruff

68. Mask

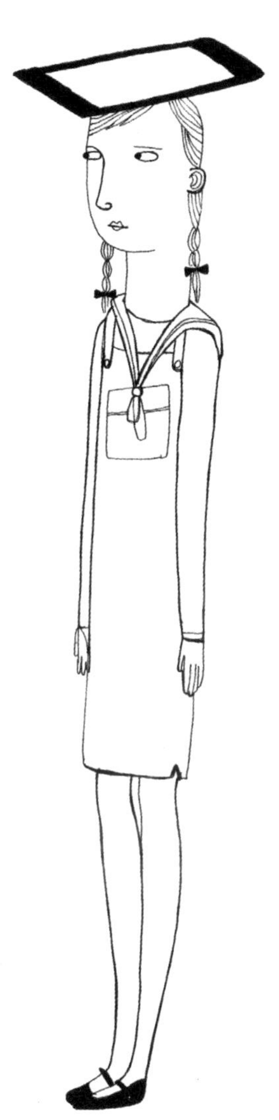

69. Deportment aid

70. Papal skull cap

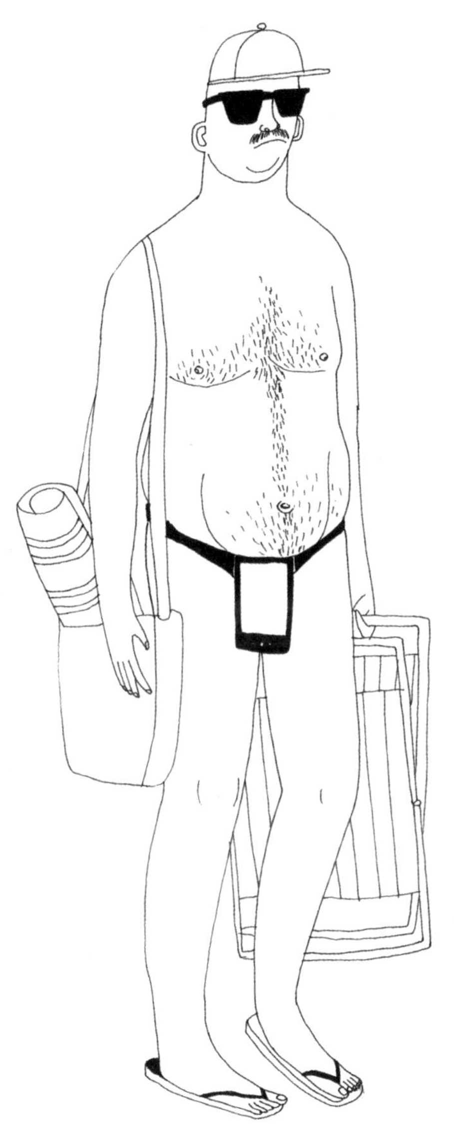

71. Speedos

72. Chastity belt

Chapter 9:
At home

73. Roof tile

74. Coaster

75. Satellite dish

76. Garden paving

77. Grouting tool

78. Teething soother

79. Drawbridge

80. Cluedo murder weapon

Chapter 10: Practical

81. iPad stand

82. Doorstop

83. Ice scraper

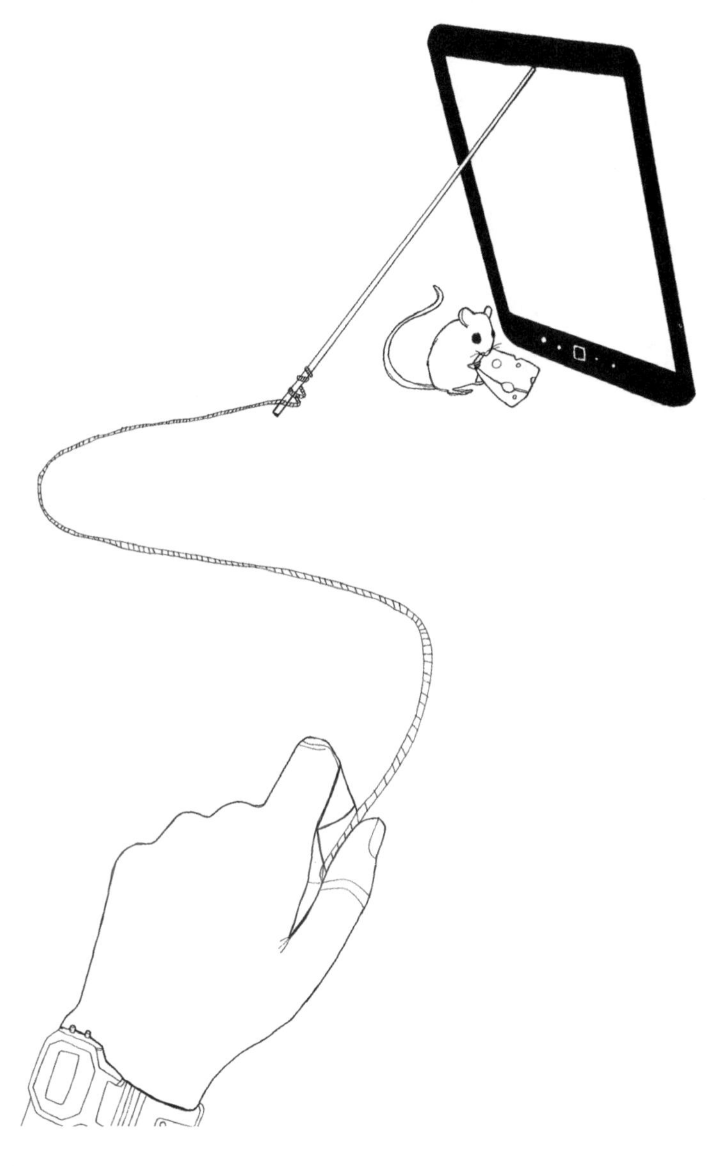

84. Mousetrap

85. Shovel

86. Demonstration placard

87. Bookmark

88. Brick

89. Fuel

90. Car mirror

91. Pick 'n' mix scoop

92. Toilet seat

Chapter 11:
Weapons and war

93. Fly-swatter

94. Sniper rifle stand

95. Tomahawk

96. Shield

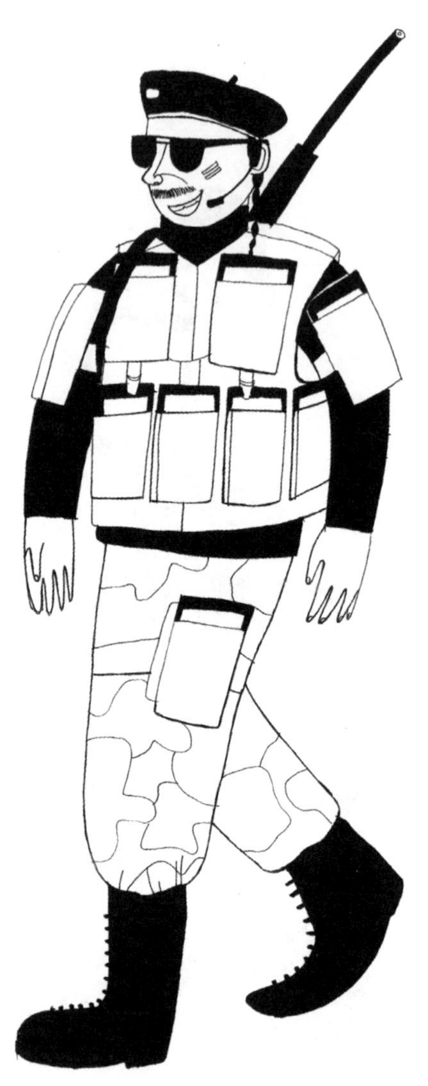

97. Body armour

98. Martial arts throwing star

Chapter 11:
Macabre

99. Meerkat club

100. Pet tombstone

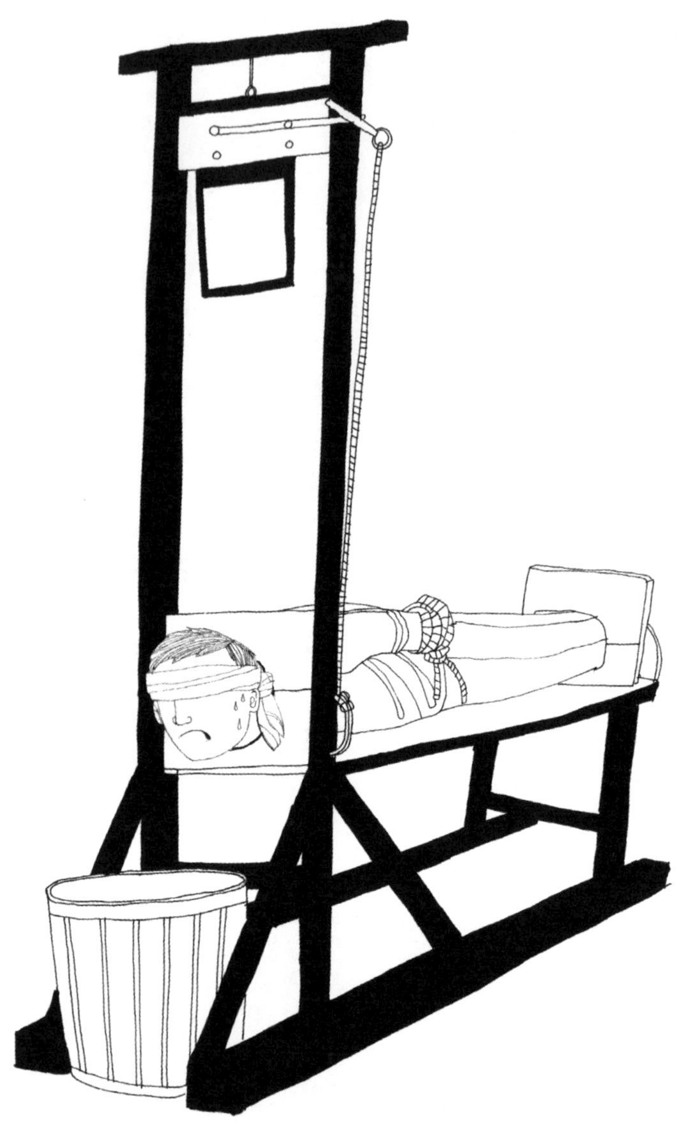

101. Guillotine